W9-BAG-556

Los Angeles
LAKERS

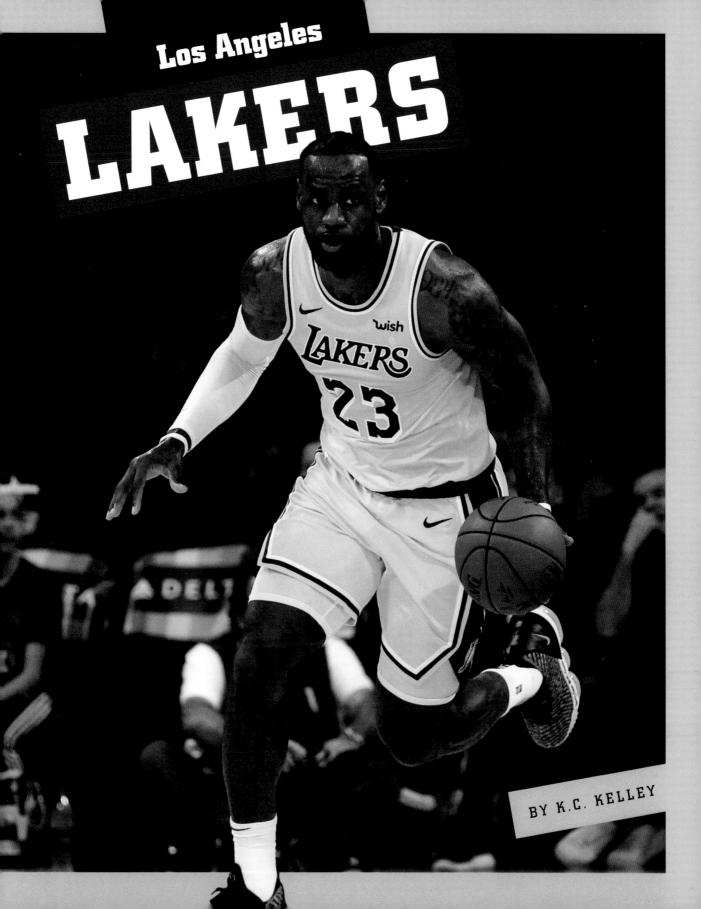

BY K.C. KELLEY

Published by The Child's World®
1980 Lookout Drive • Mankato, MN 56003-1705
800-599-READ • www.childsworld.com

Cover: © Kevin Kuo/AP Photo.
Photographs ©: AP Photo: 8, 29; Icon Sportswire 17; Matt York 25.
Alamy Photo: Sheldon Levis 12. Dreamstime.com: Juan Camilo Bernal
13. Imagn/USA Today Sports: Robert Hanashiro 26BR; Newscom: Lucy
Nicholson/Reuters 5; Brad Rempel/USA Today 6; Hector Amezcua/TNS
10; Dennis Wierzbicki/USA Today 18; John McDonough/Icon SMI 21; Jon
SooHoo/UPI 22; Roger Mallison/TNS 26TR; Kevin Kuo/USA Today 26BL.

ISBN 9781503824621
LCCN 2018964279

Printed in the United States of America
PA02416

ABOUT THE AUTHOR

K.C. Kelley is a huge sports fan who has
written more than 150 books for kids.
He has written about football, basketball,
soccer, and even auto racing! He lives in
Santa Barbara, California.

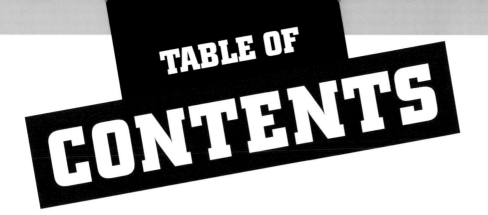

TABLE OF CONTENTS

GO, LAKERS!

Los Angeles, California, is home to lots of movie stars. It is also home to one of the most successful professional basketball teams. The Los Angeles Lakers have won 16 National Basketball Association (NBA) championships. That's the second-most ever! Let's meet this star-studded team!

Lakers star Kobe Bryant holds the 2010 NBA championship trophy. The Lakers beat the Boston Celtics. It was Los Angeles' 16th NBA title.

Superstar LeBron James joined the Lakers in 2018. He is one of the best players of all time. He hopes to lead the team back to the top!

WHO ARE THE LAKERS?

The Lakers are one of 30 NBA teams. They play in the Pacific Division of the Western Conference. The other Pacific Division teams are the Golden State Warriors, the Los Angeles Clippers, the Phoenix Suns, and the Sacramento Kings. The Lakers share the same home court as the Clippers. Their games are always tough battles!

WHERE THEY CAME FROM

There are less than a dozen lakes in Los Angeles County. So why is the basketball team called the Lakers? The team got its name from its first home. The Minneapolis Lakers started playing in 1948. Minnesota has more than 10,000 lakes! In 1960, the Lakers moved to Los Angeles. They brought the name with them.

George Mikan (99) was a star for the Minneapolis Lakers. He helped them win five NBA championships. The team moved to Los Angeles in 1960.

Brandon Ingram leaps to make a slam
He is one of the Lakers' top young play

WHO THEY PLAY

The Lakers play 82 games each season. They play 41 games at home and 41 on the road. The Lakers play four games against each of the other Pacific Division teams. They play 36 games against other Western Conference teams. The Lakers also play each of the teams in the Eastern Conference twice. That's a lot of basketball! The winner of the Western and Eastern Conferences play each other in the NBA Finals in June.

WHERE THEY PLAY

The Lakers moved into the beautiful Staples Center in 1998. It is in downtown Los Angeles. Staples is a busy place. It is also the home of the NBA's Los Angeles Clippers. The Los Angeles Kings pro hockey team plays there, too. Staples hosts concerts and award shows. Statues of Lakers heroes like Kareem Abdul-Jabbar stand outside Staples Center.

13

Fans come to Staples Center for more than just games. A busy courtyard offers restaurants and places to hear music.

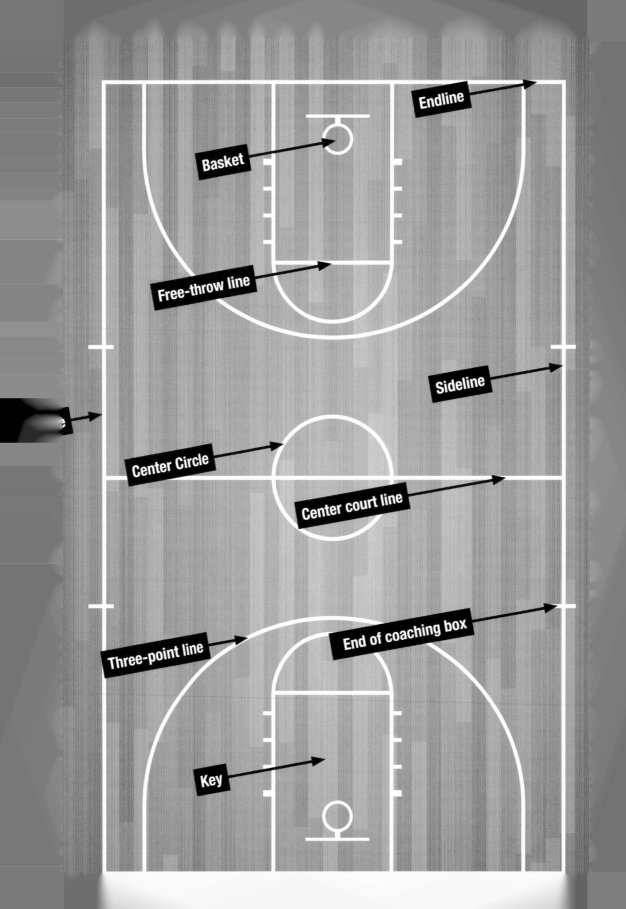

THE BASKETBALL COURT

**A**n NBA court is 94 feet long and 50 feet wide (28.6 m by 15.24 m). Nearly all the courts are made from hard maple wood. Rubber mats under the wood help make the floor springy. Each team paints the court with its logo and colors. Lines on the court show the players where to take shots. The diagram on the left shows the important parts of the NBA court.

The Staples Center court is built from 220 rectangles. It is made of maple wood. Each section is 4 feet by 8 feet (1.2 m by 2.4 m). A crew takes 90 minutes to switch from a Clippers court to a Lakers court.

The Lakers have almost always been big winners! The team won league titles in its first six seasons (1948 to 1954). In the 1980s, the Lakers won five more championships. They were led by **guard** Magic Johnson and **center** Kareem Abdul-Jabbar. Those teams used a fast style of play known as "Showtime." From 1958 until 2013, the Lakers only missed the playoffs four times. From 2000–2002, Kobe Bryant and Shaquille O'Neal led the Lakers to three NBA titles in a row.

Magic Johnson's passing skill created "Showtime." His Lakers teams ran very fast. Fans loved watching the Lakers play!

In 2014, the Lakers struggled to win games. Against the Chicago Bulls, the Lakers Jordan Howard had this shot blocked.

TOUGH TIMES

19

The Lakers have had few losing seasons. During the 1957–58 season, the team lost 53 games. That was the worst record in the league. They didn't have many other bad teams. However, starting with the 2013–14 season, the Lakers did lose a lot. They finished last four times.

ALL THE RIGHT MOVES

George Mikan was the first "big man" in NBA history. His best move was a **hook shot**. He let it go from high above his head. Later, Kareem Abdul-Jabbar used the "sky hook." His shot came from even higher than Mikan's! Magic Johnson made **no-look passes**. He looked one way and passed another. Among today's Lakers, LeBron James stars on offense. He uses his size and strength to make strong drives to the basket.

In basketball, a "big man" means a player who is tall and strong. It can also refer to a team's best player.

Kareem Abdul-Jabbar releases a sky hook. His arm held the ball way above his head. Defenders could not reach high enough to block it.

Kobe Bryant played 20 seasons with the Lakers.
He is third all-time in the NBA in scoring.

Few teams have had as many superstars as the Lakers. The first was George Mikan. He led the Lakers to five NBA titles. He also led the NBA in scoring three times. In the 1960s, Jerry West led the Lakers and played in 14 All-Star Games. Kareem Abdul-Jabbar joined the team in 1971. He won six Most Valuable Player Awards. Magic Johnson thrilled fans with his great passing and big smile. Kobe Bryant scored more points as a Laker than any other player.

HEROES NOW

LeBron James is probably the best player in basketball today. He helped the Miami Heat and Cleveland Cavaliers win NBA titles. He joined the Lakers in 2018 to help them win one, too. The Lakers also have many young players. Brandon Ingram is good on offense. Lonzo Ball is great at passing and **dribbling**. Kyle Kuzma has a great **outside shot**.

LeBron James is big, fast, and strong.
He also acts as a powerful team leader.
The Lakers are glad to have him on the team.

WHAT THEY WEAR

NBA players wear a **tank top** jersey. Players wear team shorts. Each player can choose his own sneakers. Some players also wear knee pads or wrist guards.

Each NBA team has more than one jersey style. The pictures at left show some of the Lakers' jerseys.

The NBA basketball (left) is 29.5 inches around. It is covered with leather. The leather has small bumps called pebbles.

The pebbles on a basketball help players grip it.

Here are some of the all-time career records for the Los Angeles Lakers. These stats are complete through all of the 2018–19 NBA regular season.

GAMES	
Kobe Bryant	1,346
Kareem Abdul-Jabbar	1,093

POINTS PER GAME	
Elgin Baylor	27.4
Shaquille O'Neal	27.0

ASSISTS PER GAME	
Magic Johnson	11.2
Norm Nixon	7.9

REBOUNDS PER GAME	
Wilt Chamberlain	19.2
Elgin Baylor	13.5

STEALS PER GAME	
Eddie Jones	2.1
Magic Johnson	1.9

FREE-THROW PCT.	
Cazzie Russell	.877
Sasha Vujacic	.876

JERRY WEST

29

POINTS	
Kobe Bryant	33,643
Jerry West	25,192

GLOSSARY

center *(SEN-ter)* a basketball position that plays near the basket

dribbling *(DRIB-ul-ing)* bouncing a basketball while running on the court

guard *(GARD)* a basketball position that often dribbles and passes

hook shot *(HOOK SHOT)* a way of throwing the basketball at the net from high overhead with one hand

no-look pass *(NOH-look PASS)* a pass made in one direction while the passer looks in another direction

outside shot *(OWT-side SHOT)* an attempt to make a basket taken from beyond the area near the basket

tank top *(TANK TOP)* a style of shirt that has straps over the shoulders and no sleeves

FIND OUT MORE

IN THE LIBRARY

Martin, Annabelle T. *Superstars of the Los Angeles Lakers*. Mankato, MN: Amicus, 2015.

Sports Illustrated Kids (editors). *Big Book of Who: Basketball*. New York: Sports Illustrated Kids, 2015.

Uhl, Xina M. *Kobe Bryant*. New York: Rosen Central, 2018.

ON THE WEB

Visit our website for links about the Los Angeles Lakers:
childsworld.com/links

Note to Parents, Teachers, and Librarians: We routinely verify our Web links to make sure they are safe and active sites. So encourage your readers to check them out!

INDEX